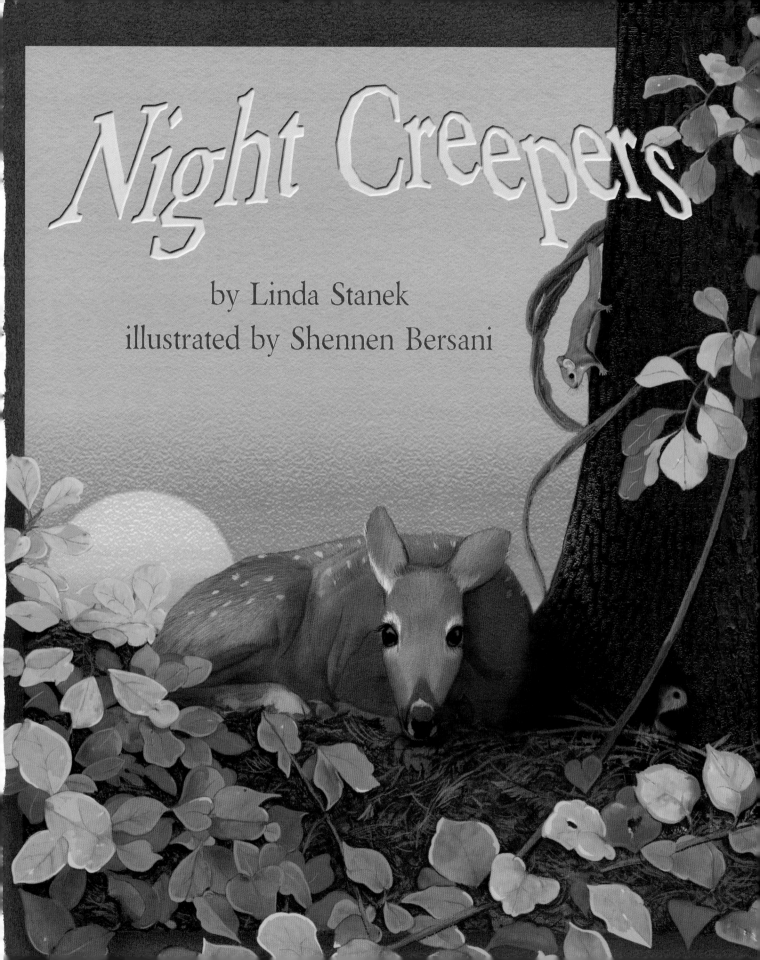

Night Creepers

by Linda Stanek

illustrated by Shennen Bersani

Waking up.

Red foxes are adaptable hunters and have a reputation for being smart and tricky.

Mother foxes, called vixens, give birth to litters of two to twelve pups in the summer. Both parents take care of their babies until their little ones are ready to venture out on their own in the fall.

Red foxes live throughout North America, Europe, Asia, and even parts of Africa.

Noisy pup.

Once gray wolves lived throughout most of North America, but they were hunted to near extinction. Now, with the help of scientists, they are making a comeback.

They live in family groups, called packs, of about eight individuals.

Wolves howl, growl, whine, and bark. Their howls can be heard miles away.

Flutter high.

Bats are the only mammals that can fly. Their arms are adapted into wings. There are over one thousand different species of bats.

Bats use echolocation to get around in the dark and find food. They make high-pitched sounds that bounce off objects around them. The sound reflects back to them (echoes) to tell them about their surroundings

Most bats eat insects, but some eat other small animals as well. Bats can also eat fruit, nectar, or even blood.

Gliding by.

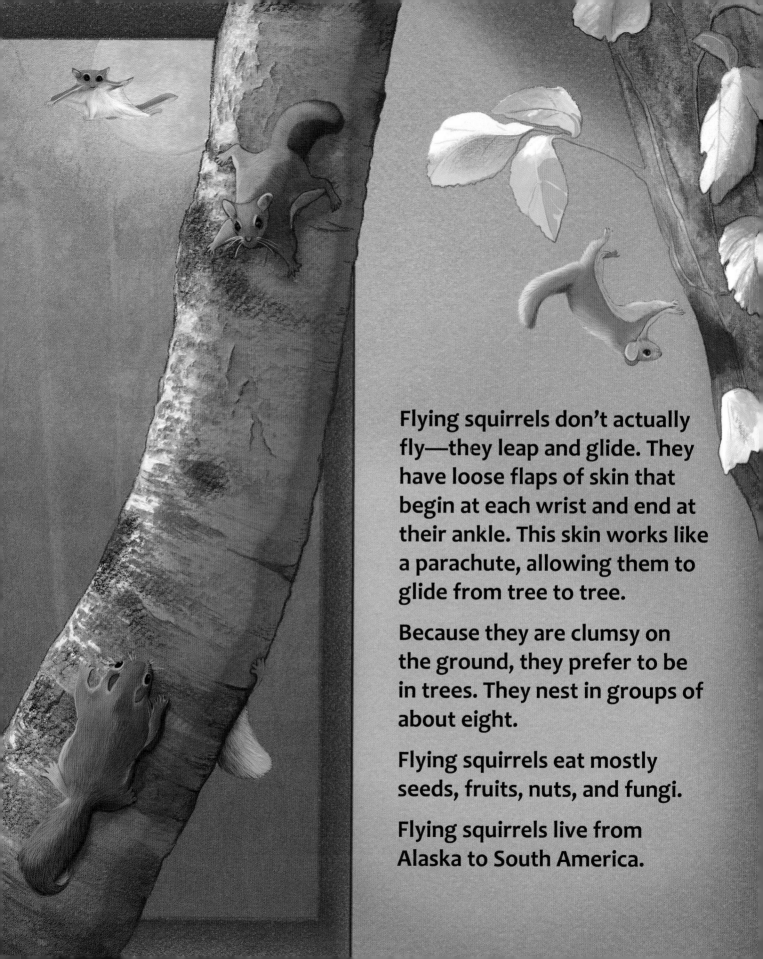

Flying squirrels don't actually fly—they leap and glide. They have loose flaps of skin that begin at each wrist and end at their ankle. This skin works like a parachute, allowing them to glide from tree to tree.

Because they are clumsy on the ground, they prefer to be in trees. They nest in groups of about eight.

Flying squirrels eat mostly seeds, fruits, nuts, and fungi.

Flying squirrels live from Alaska to South America.

Stealing food.

Skunks are famous for their foul odor. When a skunk is scared, it turns its back and sprays an awful-smelling, oily mist. Most animals will run in the other direction when sprayed.

They are opportunistic eaters because they will eat whatever food they can find. They eat worms, dead fish and animals, and plants.

Skunks live mostly in North America.

Riding brood.

Opossums are the only marsupials (pouched mammals) in North America.

A female opossum gives birth to hairless, bee-sized babies that crawl into her pouch and continue to develop. When the babies are large enough, they leave their mother's pouch. Sometimes they hitch a ride on mama's back.

Like skunks, opossums are opportunistic eaters and will often visit houses in search of food. Opossums are excellent climbers and spend a lot of time in trees. They even have a prehensile tail that can wrap around and grip, just like a hand.

PEANUT BUTTER

Croaking low.

Like all frogs, bullfrogs begin as eggs, which hatch into tadpoles, before losing their tails as they grow legs.

Male bullfrogs croak to attract females and to warn other males to stay out of their territory.

Bullfrogs hunt at night, eating anything that is small enough to fit in their mouths. This could be fish, insects, snakes, mice, turtles, and even ducklings.

Bullfrogs live throughout North and South America.

Blink and glow.

Fireflies are sometimes called lightning bugs. There are about two thousand types of fireflies in the world. Each species has a unique blink. Some blink fast and some blink slow. Some groups all blink at the same time.

Fireflies have chemicals in their body that help to make them glow. This is called bioluminescence, which means "light from life." This light attracts mates, and warns bug-eaters to stay away—fireflies don't taste good.

They live in most of North and South America, as well as Europe and Asia.

Wash and clean.

Raccoons eat almost anything. They snag food from streams, grab eggs from nests, eat plants and fruits, and catch mice and insects for food.

Raccoons are smart. They can use their well-developed front paws to open simple locks and get into trashcans. Raccoons eat all they can during the summer and sleep through much of the winter. Raccoons live in much of North and Central America.

Poke and preen.

Owls are famous for their excellent night vision, and their hearing is almost as good. An owl can hear a mouse snap a twig seventy-five feet away.

Owls don't have eye muscles to look around with. Instead, they must move their heads. This gives owls better focus.

Owls' feathers have soft edges that allow them to fly silently. Like other birds, they use their beaks to smooth and arrange their feathers. This is called "preening."

Bedding down. Shhh . . .

Not a sound.

Bobcats are solitary animals that live alone. Bobcats live together when a mom is raising her babies, or when young brothers and sisters are not quite ready to be on their own.

Bobcats are named for their tails, which look "bobbed," or cut short. Bobcats are about twice the size of a housecat, but these tough felines can bring down a deer.

They live from southern Canada to Central America.

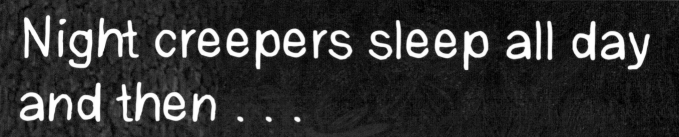

Night creepers sleep all day and then . . .

White-tailed deer mothers are called does. They leave their napping babies alone during the day to prevent predators from noticing them.

White-tailed deer live from southern Canada to northern South America.

. . . it's time for them
to creep again.

For Creative Minds

When They're Most Active

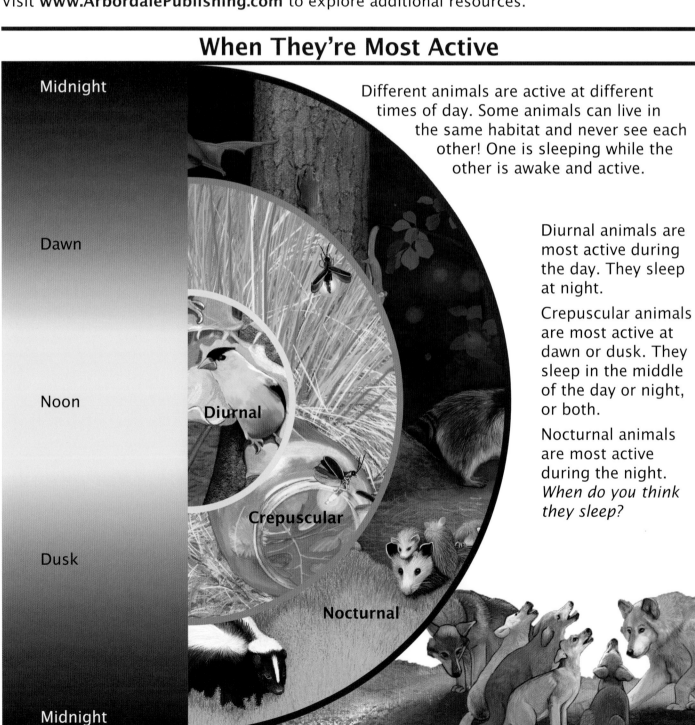

Different animals are active at different times of day. Some animals can live in the same habitat and never see each other! One is sleeping while the other is awake and active.

Diurnal animals are most active during the day. They sleep at night.

Crepuscular animals are most active at dawn or dusk. They sleep in the middle of the day or night, or both.

Nocturnal animals are most active during the night. *When do you think they sleep?*

Sorting

Sort the following animals into three groups: nocturnal, diurnal, and crepuscular. Read the animal fun facts for clues. Answers are below.

The barn owl only hunts at night.

People are mostly active during daytime hours.

Bats use sound (echolocation) to find their way in the dark.

Skunks scavenge for food primarily in the twilight hours at sunrise and sunset.

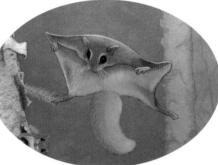

Flying squirrels in North America are active while people are sleeping.

Fireflies are normally seen at nightfall.

Like housecats, bobcats are mostly active in the early morning and evening hours.

Nocturnal: barn owls, bats, flying squirrels
Diurnal: people
Crepuscular: skunks, fireflies, bobcats

Animal Adaptations

 Like many nocturnal animals, flying squirrels have large eyes. The pupil is the dark circle in the center of the eye. In bright light, the pupil shrinks to not let in too much light. When it is dark, the pupil widens. This lets more light enter the eye. Flying squirrels' large eyes help them see in the dark.

Fireflies have a special light organ. They use a chemical reaction inside their bodies to make them light up (bioluminescence). Fireflies use their lights to find and communicate with other fireflies. Fireflies also make chemicals in their bodies that make them taste bad to predators. The light reminds other animals that fireflies are not a good meal.

 Barn owls are birds of prey. They hunt other animals for food. Owls' feathers have a soft front edge. These special feathers make almost no noise as the owl flies. An owl's prey usually can't hear the owl swooping overhead.

Bats use their ears to map their surroundings. They squeak and listen for echoes. Some bats have large ears that can move independently of each other. The sound of an echo tells the bat the size and shape of objects nearby. This is a type of echolocation.

 Frogs don't have thumbs to pick up their food; they use their tongues instead. The long tongue flicks out, so fast it can be hard to see. When it touches an insect, the bug sticks to the tongue and the frog has a tasty snack.

On this page are two mammals, one bird, one amphibian, and one insect. Can you tell which is which?

Match the Eyes

In many nocturnal animals, light is not absorbed by the eye. It is reflected by it. This is called **eyeshine**. Light enters the eye and bounces off a special, mirror-like membrane (tapetum). This helps the animal see in the dark. They can see by the light coming into their eyes *and* by the light reflecting out.

Small amounts of light (like starlight and moonlight) or bright lights (like a fire or the headlights of a car) are reflected, making it look like the eyes glow in the dark. Different animals' eyes glow different colors. Match the eyeshine below to the animal it comes from.

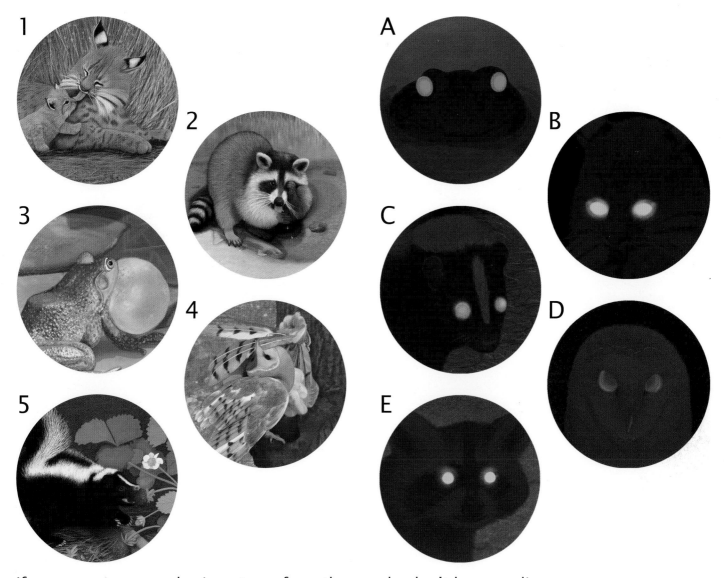

If you ever see eyes glowing at you from the woods, don't be scared!
There are no monsters there, only night creepers.

Answers: 1B - bobcat. 2E - raccoon. 3A - bullfrog. 4D - barn owl. 5C - skunk.

To my husband Ken~my heart, my joy, and my partner in all.—LS

To research these illustrations, I got outdoors. I found many of this book's creepers while on a trip to Alaska far from my home at the Anchorage Zoo. I found most of the animals back in Massachusetts at the Stone Zoo in Stoneham, the Mass Audubon's Blue Hills Trailside Museum in Milton, and the wooded areas surrounding my home in Wayland, MA. Many of these animals can be found in your own backyard at night. I dedicate this book in memory of my Mother, Elsie McNeil, who created a passion in me for animals of all kinds.—SB

Thanks to Kenneth Rainer, Education Coordinator at the GTM Research Reserve, and Cathleen McConnell, Community and Guest Engagement, Point Defiance Zoo & Aquarium, for verifying the accuracy of the information in this book.

Library of Congress Cataloging-in-Publication Data

Names: Stanek, Linda, author. | Bersani, Shennen, illustrator.
Title: Night creepers / by Linda Stanek ; illustrated by Shennen Bersani.
Description: Mount Pleasant, SC : Arbordale Publishing, [2017] | Audience: K to grade 3.
Identifiers: LCCN 2017018952 (print) | LCCN 2017026584 (ebook) | ISBN 9781607183266 (English Downloadable eBook) | ISBN 9781607183563 (English Interactive Dual-Language eBook) | ISBN 9781607183273 (Spanish Downloadable eBook) | ISBN 9781607183570 (Spanish Interactive Dual-Language eBook) | ISBN 9781607183228 (english hardcover) | ISBN 9781607183235 (english pbk.) | ISBN 9781607183259 (spanish pbk.)
Subjects: LCSH: Nocturnal animals--Juvenile literature. | Animal behavior--Juvenile literature.
Classification: LCC QL755.5 (ebook) | LCC QL755.5 .S73 2017 (print) | DDC 591.5/18--dc23
LC record available at https://lccn.loc.gov/2017018952

Translated into Spanish: *Sigilosos de la noche*

Lexile® Level: 780L
key phrases: nocturnal, crepuscular, animal adaptations
Animals in this book include red fox, wolf, bat, flying squirrel, skunk, opossum, bullfrog, firefly, racoon, owl, bobcat, and white-tailed deer.

Manufactured in China, June 2017
This product conforms to CPSIA 2008
First Printing

Arbordale Publishing
Mt. Pleasant, SC 29464
www.ArbordalePublishing.com